RACQUETBALL BASICS:
HOW TO PLAY RACQUETBALL

Lisa Mallon

I dedicate this book to every person – who has been lucky enough to have their lives touched by the joy, excitement and sheer buzz of racquetball...

Contents

The History of Racquetball

Racquetball is an indoor sport that's played with a hollow rubber ball.

It is often likened to handball and tennis, owing to the fact that many aspects of these two sports were adopted in developing the sport of racquetball.

Despite the similarities, though, racquetball has evolved into a totally separate and unmatched sport on its own.

Professional tennis and handball player Joe Sobek is credited for developing the sport back in 1950. He is said to have introduced the game for the very first time at the Greenwich YMCA, although he hasn't thought of a good name for the game at the time.

The new game resulted from his search for a sport that's both rapid and easy to learn. It thus became a good alternative to tennis.

Two years later, Sobek founded the National Paddle Rackets Association (NPRA). In the same year, he codified the mechanics of the new game he invented and then had them printed in a booklet.

As a result, many people quickly adopted the new sport and it gradually became one of the more popular indoor sports of the time.

The game's popularity grew even more with continued promotion until it gained the support of as much as 40,000 handball courts in the YMCAs and JCCs, where it can be appropriately played.

The International Racquetball Association (IRA), however, wasn't established until 1969, which was also when the new sport got its name, as coined by Bob McInerney, a professional tennis player.

On that same year, the Association assumed the roles of the NPRA. In 1973, however, the directors of the IRA and Robert W. Kendler, president and founder of the United States Handball Association, had a major dispute.

As a result of this dispute, Kendler formed two new organisations for racquetball.

Over the years, though, the IRA has maintained its dominance as the primary organisation promoting the sport of racquetball.

No less than the United States Olympic Committee recognised the IRA as the national governing body for the sport in the country.

Racquetball's peak in popularity was seen in the year 1974, when an estimated three million players were said to be engaged in the sport in the United States alone.

During that same year, the IRA organised the very first professional racquetball tournament.

The same organisation then proceeded to become one of the founding members of the International Racquetball Federation (IRF).

These developments marked the spreading of the sport's popularity to several different parts of the world.

A number of clubs and courts were built and founded over the years as a result of racquetball's growing popularity. Several sporting goods manufacturers also started selling racquetball equipment.

The sport kept growing in popularity until the early 1980s, after which it suffered a decline in popularity as racquet clubs started being converted into health clubs due to the changing demands at the time.

It regained some of its popularity by the early 1990s, when the estimated number of players in the United States alone went above five million.

Today, sports fanatics have welcomed racquetball, especially in the United Kingdom, which makes it still one of the world's most popular sports.

Why Choose Racquetball?

In an effort to maintain good physical and mental health, people tend to try all sorts of exercise programs and routines.

There are those who jog regularly, swim, or spend hours lifting weights at the gym.

Other people choose to play football, basketball, or soccer.

There are also those who've found joy in something more unique and relatively young as a sport – racquetball.

The sport is considered young because it was developed just a little more than 50 years ago.

If you've never played racquetball before, then you may be wondering just what it is that people find so exciting about this sport.

To put it simply, racquetball effectively stimulates your mind, energizes your body, and gives your spirit a much-needed lift.

There are few other sports that can successfully provide you with such an exhilarating experience.

Consider what the game does for your mind. Every single play you execute requires quick judgment and reaction time as well as skilled precision.

When you play racquetball, it's as if you're giving your mind one strenuous activity after another.

Such a challenge will undoubtedly keep your brain young and healthy.

Even when you're standing still in anticipation of your opponent's serve, you'll have to maintain mental alertness so you'll know how to react.

When you play regularly, you'll soon find that this kind of mental stimulation can positively affect several areas of your life, including your work or studies and even some of the most mundane tasks you regularly perform.

In the same way your mind is stimulated, your body also gains a lot of benefits from the intense movements required to become a good racquetball player.

The tasks of making a dive, turning quickly to the right, moving swiftly to the left, jumping, swinging from just about every possible angle, can all result in giving your muscle groups a good amount of healthy stress.

The constant going up and down the court and moving from left to right is generally equivalent to a really long running or jogging session.

Your blood flows, your muscles are effectively stretched, and your whole body is energized. This is definitely more than you can ever hope to achieve with other sports.

Aside from the mental and physical benefits, racquetball also effectively lifts your spirits. One of the primary reasons for this is the interaction that naturally occurs between players.

There may be times when you'll have to play against a complete stranger, but this sport is mostly played among friends or at least acquaintances who soon become friends.

The racquetball court is, in fact, often thought of as a sort of social meeting place.

After playing an energetic round of racquetball, players usually leave refreshed. Their moods are also lifted and their attitudes renewed.

The racquetball experience, therefore, provides you with the same kind of satisfaction you normally get from a pleasant and encouraging conversation with your peers.

So, there's absolutely no reason for you not to take advantage of the opportunity to learn this sport and share in its joys.

The Right Equipment

Racquetball is one sport that can easily be enjoyed by one, two, or four players at a time and many people consider it an excellent way to release some of the frustration brought on by school or work.

It can also be a great bonding activity for the family as the task of bouncing the ball on the walls and running into each other while doing so often leads to a good deal of laughter and promotes a feeling of togetherness not only during the game itself, but also when you recall the fun later at dinnertime.

To avoid conflicts, though, you should be careful not to hold games where parents play against their kids.

For one thing, this would cause the kids to argue over whose turn it is to serve or hit the ball.

Whatever your purpose is for playing racquetball – whether to bond with your family, pass the time with friends, or in preparation for going pro – you'll need to use specific equipment so you can play properly.

The first on your list should be protective eyewear.

Remember to choose one that fits snugly onto your face, especially if you wear glasses.

This saves you from costly repairs for broken glasses and keeps your eyes safe in case your face gets hit with the ball.

Obviously, another piece of equipment you'll need is the racquet, which differentiates the game from handball.

Be sure to choose a racquet that fits your hand well enough without feeling too heavy.

If you're playing for fitness or recreation purposes, then you may want to settle for a good racquet that costs around $60, but if you plan to go pro, then a professional-grade racquet that costs around $200 would be a better choice.

If you don't plan to play that often, then you could perhaps borrow a racquet from your local YMCA.

Other than the racquet and protective eyewear, you should also choose between two sizes of grips for your racquet.

You may check with your local sporting goods store to find out which grip size is right for you.

Of course, using the right pair of shoes is also an important consideration when playing racquetball.

Take note that it's not advisable to wear cross trainers or running shoes in this case, as they lack the necessary support for your feet.

You need to choose gum-soled shoes that have better grip on the floor and you need to make sure the shoes don't twist or buckle under pressure.

You may also want to choose hard soles to prevent rolling your ankles.

Another important piece of equipment is a pair of gloves, as they help you grip the racquet and aim better.

You'll also need to have replacement strings at the ready, as you never know when you're going to need them.

In order to buy the right string, it's best to bring your racquet to the local sporting goods store and then ask a sales representative for assistance.

Most importantly, you'll need to buy balls and in doing so, you'll have to consider whether you'll be playing indoors or outdoors, as there are different balls for each type of racquetball court.

Choosing a Ball

When you go out to shop for racquetball balls, you just might get confused by the number of differently-coloured balls out there.

You may even be asking yourself if the colour matters.

Surprisingly, yes.

And in order to take away the confusion, let me explain:

1. Blue Balls

Blue is the standard colour for racquetball balls. A blue ball, therefore, will have average speed and bounce.

The usual brands of blue balls are Penn, Ektelon, and ProKennex.

The blue balls from all of these brands are known to have similar speeds, although they differ a bit in the amount of bounce.

ProKennex and Ektelon balls are believed to have more bounce, but it is the Penn Ultra-Blue ball that's currently the most popular among recreational racquetball players.

2. Red Balls

There are generally two brands and models for red racquetball balls, and these are the Ektelon Fireball and the Penn Ballistic 2.0. ProKennex also offers a ball with similar attributes, but has it in Orange.

The red balls are said to be the fastest and heaviest balls of their kind.

Owing to their speed and bright colour, they're generally considered ideal for outdoor games. The World Outdoor Racquetball (WOR) has chosen the Ektelon Fireball as the official ball for its games.

3. Purple and Green Balls

Penn offers purple and green racquetball balls in their Pro Penn line. These balls are known to be much faster than blue balls, but not quite as fast as red balls. These are quite lively balls and they've become part of the standard equipment at most sanctioned tournaments currently in existence.

A lot of racquetball players prefer the purple balls because of their enhanced visibility on the racquetball court. In fact, the International Racquetball Tour (IRT) has chosen the Pro Penn HD purple ball as the official ball for its games.

4. Black Balls

These are classic balls offered by Ektelon that emulate the older style of the sport. These balls are generally slower, softer, and lighter than the other balls.

Playing with this ball often leads to much longer rallies and it is more popular among senior racquetball players.

The Classic Pro Racquetball Tour (CPRT) has chosen the Ektelon Classic Black ball as the official ball for its games.

So, now you have a better understanding of what the colours signify in racquetball balls.

You should also have a general idea now as to which particular ball best suits your playing style.

It may be a good idea to start playing with the type of ball that conforms to your style of play best.

However, you may want to challenge yourself in the future by playing with a different type of ball.

Varying the game and constantly challenging yourself is an excellent way of keeping the sport interesting and the racquetball experience fun.

If, after reading this section, you still aren't quite sure which ball you should start playing with, it may be wise for you to visit your local sporting goods store and ask for assistance from their sales representative.

Choosing a Racquet

The task of choosing a racquetball racquet can be a bit tricky.

If you're buying a racquet for the very first time, then it may be a good idea to ask yourself the following questions before you go shopping:

1. What's Your Grip Size?

If you normally wear an XL glove, then you'd best choose an XS grip.

Most players go for SS grips, though, as this allows them to easily move the racquet around in their hands.

The smaller grip also allows for more control and more wrist snap, which results in giving more power to your shots.

If you're not quite sure what grip size to choose, it's safe to go with the SS, as it can be easy to increase the size with tape later on if you feel the need to do so.

Take note as well that there are rounder grips than others, so you may want to test a few models to see which one feels most comfortable in your hands.

2. What Weight are You Looking for?

Good racquets generally weigh 150-195 grams. Take note that more advanced players often choose lighter racquets because it provides them with more control, as it is a lot easier to manoeuvre.

Almost all professional racquetball players use racquets that weigh 170-175 grams. Racquets within this range allow you to move around easily while still generating a significant amount of force.

Heavier racquets generally provide you with more power, which makes them ideal for players with slower swing speeds. The drawback is that it can also lead to more arm fatigue.

3. Is That All There is to It?

You're not quite done yet, as there are still factors such as balance and swing weight to consider.

Balance helps describe the distribution of weight in the racquet. A head heavy racquet has the centre of its mass towards the head.

Take note that mass that's further away from your hand generates more power, but mass that's closer to your hand provides you with more control.

Swing weight refers to how heavy the racquet feels when you swing it. It is defined as the combination of balance and the racquet's actual weight.

4. What about Durability?

The good news is that you shouldn't really have a problem with durability as long as you don't smash your racquet against a wall, as most of the racquets available today have been manufactured using modern technologies.

It's also good to know most modern racquets are offered with a one-year warranty in case you do smash it against the wall by accident.

Yes, choosing the right racquet can be a little tricky. But, as long as you take note of the answers to the questions posed above, you should find the task a lot easier and much less overwhelming.

If you're still unsure by the time you get to your local sporting goods store, then you may as well ask for the assistance of any of their sales representatives so you can make a better informed decision.

Racquetball Rules

Racquetball owes a large part of its popularity to the simplicity of its nature as well as its rules.

If you're planning to take up this sport, then you should definitely learn the basic rules of the game.

Single, Double, or Trio

Racquetball may be played by two players against each other, by four players with two players on each team, or with three players with every player playing against the other two.

The player who serves the ball is the only one who can score a point. In case he loses the serve, it's called a sideout.

In a doubles game, both players on a team should serve before a sideout is called. Whoever wins two games (race to 15 per game) first wins the match.

Courts and Racquets

The four-walled racquetball court is 40 feet in length and 20 feet wide, with a 20-foot ceiling height.

There are markers that indicate where the receiving area, serving boxes, and serving area are.

These markers are known as the receiving line, drive serve line, service line, and short line.

Racquets used in the sport are equipped with bumper guards and grips that have nylon ropes to secure the racquet to your wrist. Racquetball players are also required to use protective eyewear during a game.

Game Proper

A game officially begins with a coin toss, with the winner being given the chance to choose whether to serve or receive first.

The roles are then switched in the next round, with the initial server becoming the receiver.

Whoever scores the most number of points in the first two games gets the chance to choose who serves in a tiebreaker.

In case there's an equal number of points, a coin toss will once again be done.

In recreational games, though, players will normally offer the decision to the other player as a sign of courtesy.

More Rules

When serving, you need to stand in the service area and step on the line without passing beyond it.

Once the ball has passed the short line, you may also pass. Take note that there has to be a continual motion throughout a serve and the receiver has to let the ball bounce once before hitting it.

In a doubles game, only one player from the serving team gets to serve on the first serve.

After that, each player on the team serves before the team is called for a sideout.

The non-serving player will have to stand with his back against the side wall and both of his feet on the ground.

He should move only when the ball passes the short line.

Rallies and Hinders

A rally shall remain in force until any of the following occurs: a player is called for carrying the ball, the ball gets hit out of court, the ball fails to reach the front wall, or the ball bounces twice before the receiver could successfully hit it.

If a hinder occurs, the serve or play is deemed over. Hinders are comprised of moves such as a screen, a holdup, or a court hinder.

After learning about the game rules, you should now be confident enough to start playing racquetball.

How to Execute the Right Grip

If you've been playing another racquet sport for some time, particularly one that requires the use of a longer racquet, then you most probably have to adjust your grip when you start playing racquetball.

Before you even engage in your first racquetball game, you'll have to make sure you have the right expectations as regards the correct racquetball grip.

When playing racquetball, take note that you have to hold the racquet such that your hand extends to a point below the end of the racquet's grip.

You should also make sure that your little finger is held entirely below the grip.

This may seem more than a little weird or even a bit uncomfortable at first, and it may even cause you to lose your control over the racquet head, but there's actually a good reason for gripping the racquet in this manner when playing racquetball.

The fact is that a racquetball racquet is just too short for you to hold the way you would a racquet for another sport.

By holding it much lower down than usual, you can effectively lengthen the racquet and achieve more pace in your shots.

Take note as well that a good racquetball player uses a good amount of wrist snap when he makes contact with the ball.

This is one of the major advantages of the extended grip, as it allows for an unimpeded movement of your wrist as well as the use of the full range of its natural motion.

Since the base of your palm is touching the butt of the racquet handle, the butt cannot bump against your wrist to impede its movement.

In order to achieve the correct grip in racquetball, you need to hold the racquet by its throat with your non-hitting hand. The aim is to hold the face of the racquet perpendicular to the floor.

The next step is for you to "shake hands" with the racquet such that the base of the V that's formed by your forefinger and thumb is positioned right at the centre of the racquet's grip.

You should then slide your hand down the length of the grip until your little finger no longer touches the grip and the butt of the grip is positioned against the base of your palm. The good thing about this grip is that it works effectively for both forehand and backhand shots. If you feel the need to adjust your grip in the course of the game, you may move the V to the right or left.

One thing you have to make sure of is that your little finger extends all the way below the butt of the racquet's grip.

Since there's a good chance that your grip will shift a lot in the course of the game and that the butt of the grip will constantly rub against your palm, it's advisable to wear a pair of gloves that's especially designed for racquetball so you can avoid suffering from blisters.

As with just about anything else, practicing the right grip will make you more comfortable with it in the long run.

How to Hit a Lob Serve

Racquetball is known for quick ball movement and a generally fast game pace. It does, however, have several elements taken from slower sports.

In fact, there's a very effective way of slowing down the game, and that's by delivering a lob serve.

Here's how to successfully execute a lob serve and consequently slow down the pace of the game:

1. Just like any other sport, a good serve in racquetball requires great positioning. There's no need to rush through your serve, since a rally can't begin until the ball is served, anyway. Make sure you're properly balanced and prepared to hit the perfect serve.

2. Make sure you stand right in the centre of the service box, whether you're planning to set your opponent up for a forehand or a backhand serve. The point at which the ball bounces off the front wall is affected when you stand too far to one side.

The ball just might hit the side wall and give your opponent the perfect opportunity for a kill shot.

3. Strive to make the ball bounce at about head height by simply dropping it. If the ball bounces too low, you're likely to hit it with too much power, thus delivering a serve that bounces too far off the back wall. If it bounces too high, you're likely to hit the ball too lightly.

4. The key to a successful lob serve is ball positioning and the speed with which it bounces off of the front wall. Your aim in serving is to push the ball and take off a significant amount of speed while giving it a good bounce. As the ball reaches its peak, you should turn your hips and body to push the ball towards the wall. When you use your arm, the serve will have too much power.

5. When you hit the ball, you should aim about ¾ up the wall towards the right or left such that it hugs the sidewall after hitting the front wall.

After hugging the side wall, the ball should hit just before the encroachment line and head towards either of the back corners without hitting the back wall. When you leave the ball in the centre of the court, your opponent can take just about any shot he wants.

6. Be sure to hold the racquet with a firm wrist, as this eliminates the possibility of delivering a flimsy serve and allows you to hit a more accurate and precise shot.

7. Take note that a lob serve isn't meant to be a difficult serve and a fault that occurs when delivering this type of serve is usually the result of rushing, nervousness, or simply being lazy. It's advisable for you to take a deep breath and make sure this serve counts.

Many players prefer delivering a lob serve because it requires much less energy. This is important, since a racquetball rally tends to take a significant amount of energy from you.

This type of serve is also associated with a high success rate, which may be why it's very popular among players of any skill level.

Racquetball Defense

Just like many other sports, a good defense is very important in achieving success in racquetball.

This refers to the series of moves you make in response to the offensive moves of your opponent.

Here are some useful tips for developing a good racquetball defense:

1. Focus Court

The middle court is generally considered as the strongest position in racquetball.

When you're in the middle court, you can be on top of every aspect of the game.

You're placed in a defensive position when your opponent is occupying that space and you need to do what you can to take the position.

You can successfully take your opponent out of the focus court by hitting a pass shot or a ceiling shot. Try to stay away from the side walls, as that can result in your opponent dominating the court.

2. Pass Shot

This shot is considered a very good defensive shot in racquetball and the good thing about it is that practically anyone can execute it successfully, regardless of your skill level.

Your aim is to hit the ball towards the front wall such that it comes as far away from your opponent as possible. Try to hit the ball as fast as you can in order to optimize this defensive shot.

3. Kill Shot

The aim of this shot is to hit the ball really low off of the front wall without letting it hit the side walls.

When you execute this shot perfectly, you can make the ball bounce twice very quickly, thus making it impossible for your opponent to return.

The best way to execute this shot is to hit the ball just a couple of inches from the floor and straight towards the front wall.

4. Z-ball Shot

This shot hits the front wall first and then one side wall before it hits the other side wall and returns parallel to the back wall.

As the ball travels from one wall to the next, it successfully gathers adequate spin. If you're able to execute it correctly, the ball should roll alongside the court's back wall, thus making it very difficult for your opponent to return.

5. Around the World

When you find yourself out of position, you can still execute a defensive shot, provided that you execute it with adequate force.

What you need to do is hit the ball into one of the side walls with enough force to give it the kind of momentum that will make it rebound on the front wall.

After rebounding, the ball should still have enough energy to hit the other side wall as high up as possible. The ball should then bounce almost behind the centre court and head to the other back corner. It will then hit the back corner wall and make a second bounce.

These are the basic defensive moves you should practice as a beginner in the sport.

Take note, however, that most of the professional players make use of other defensive moves that include a combination of the above techniques as well as a few variations.

Just like many other sports, a good defense can be your best offense in racquetball.

Improving Your Ceiling Game

If you aim to win every racquetball game you play, then you'll have to add a good ceiling game to your arsenal.

This is one defensive strategy used by many players to get their opponent away from the centre court.

The general rule is for you to hit this shot when you're not in the position to hit a good offensive shot.

The intention is to force your opponent to shoot from the back court, which is where most mistakes occur.

Here are three effective ways of improving your ceiling game in racquetball:

1. Hit Ceiling Shots during Warm-up

After getting your stretching out of the way, it's a good idea to continue warming up by hitting ceiling shots.

Warm up your shoulder by repeatedly hitting the ball to the ceiling.

This is important because stepping on the court and playing without a proper warm-up can be bad news for you muscles.

Warming up with ceiling shots helps you avoid muscle injury and develop your ceiling game at the same time.

Remember to practice your backhand as much as your forehand to increase your confidence in your skills. It's best to engage in this drill for five minutes.

2. Spend At Least 15 Minutes Each Week Practicing Your Ceiling Game

As with almost anything else, constant practice helps you get better at hitting ceiling shots.

By spending as little as 15 minutes each week practicing your ceiling shots, you should be able to achieve much-needed consistency.

You may do this on a single day each week or in 5-minute sessions three times a week.

3. Offensive and Defensive Drills

There are a number of offensive and defensive drills you can do to improve your ceiling game. One such drill is to play short games (race to five) where scores are awarded in every rally.

This drill can effectively help you build strength and endurance, as a result of long rallies that truly test your arms and legs. Another drill you can do either at a practice game or an actual competition is to try to beat your opponent by hitting purely ceiling shots.

You may not be able to hit ceiling shots all the time, but you should strive to do so about 90% of the time.

That is to say, you should hit ceiling shots repeatedly until your opponent invariably provides you with an opportunity to hit a good offensive shot to win the rally.

Of course, you're likely to experience a bit of an adjustment period as you practice hitting ceiling shots and gradually learn what your strong and weak points are.

Soon enough, you should learn how to take advantage of your strong points and improve on your weak points.

To begin with, though, it's a good idea to focus on ceilings and to keep hitting ceiling shots until your opponent gives you the perfect offensive opening you surely can't miss.

The three tips discussed above should be enough to help you improve your ceiling game and have you looking forward to taking your racquetball game to the next level.

How to Win

What does it take for you to win at racquetball? Is it the right equipment?

Is it an advanced set of skills? Is it a good strategy?

The truth is that it takes a good combination of all these, along with a competitive spirit, to win a racquetball game.

Although there are varying opinions as regards the amount of emphasis that each component should be given, everybody agrees that all of these components deserve serious consideration from those who truly want to excel at this sport.

Let's take equipment, for one thing. Modern technology has introduced a number of changes in the way racquetball equipment is manufactured.

The subtle differences in the size and weight of the racquet, the shape of the frame, and the concavity can all play a role in increasing your chances of winning.
Furthermore, the gauge of the racquet string helps determine the control and power with which you hit the ball.

It also plays an important role in the durability of the string itself.

For its part, a racquetball glove allows you to maintain a better grip on the racquet. And the type of ball you choose to play with also affects your game, since balls are made with differing weights, speeds, and visibility.

What about skill and strategy? Skills are generally related to your strength, agility, and dexterity.

Remember that a game of racquetball requires you to quickly move forwards, backwards, or laterally. This means you should have a good eyesight, quick reaction times, and excellent judgment so you can be in the right position at the right instances during a game.

As for strategy, you need to understand that this is something that generally comes with time. The best way to develop excellent technique and strategy is to play with experienced players and learn from them.

You may also want to watch training videos and read up on racquetball strategies. While there are some players who seem to have a natural talent for strategizing, most require a great deal of time to master this aspect of the game.

Of course, knowing how to win at racquetball is one thing and actually winning games is another. This means it's not enough to have all of this information; you'll have to put the information to good use.

Perhaps the best way to make use of the information that you have is to constantly practice your strategies in order to master them and enhance your skills at the same time. The more frequently you train your muscles in the usual movements used in a racquetball game, the more you'll develop your ability to react promptly, move quickly, and make proper judgments.

Since all good strategies begin in the brain, training your neural pathways is also a very effective way of improving your racquetball skills.

Now you should be ready to put this combination of strategy, skill, and good equipment to use.

When coupled with a natural love for the sport and a healthy competitive spirit, this should help you become the best racquetball player that you can possibly be.

And you can finally look forward to winning all those racquetball games.

What NOT to Do in Racquetball

As much as you need to learn what you should do to become a good racquetball player and win all those racquetball games, you also need to learn the things you should avoid doing when playing the sport.

Here's a list of racquetball "dont's" that should serve as your guide to enjoying the game even more:

1. Don't move backwards as you swing. Rather, you should step forward and pull your hips with your legs as you rotate. Make sure you're always ahead of the ball so you can step forward as you take your set-up position.

2. Don't begin your forward swing exclusively with your arms and hands, as this will reduce the power of the swing.

3. Don't straighten one knee while bending the other. When you bend your knees, make sure both of them are bent.

4. Don' move your shoulders and hips in a straight line.

Rather, you should make sure they rotate in a circular motion, beginning with the hips and then moving on to the shoulders.

5. Don't place any tension on your arms. Be sure to hold them limp and loose as you prepare for a shot.

6. Don't force your muscles to work in case you fail to hit the ball sufficiently hard. What you need to do instead is analyze your swing and determine where you lose power and why the power doesn't reach your arms and wrists.

7. Don't lose your balance after the swing. If you do, then you should review the sequence of your moves.

8. Don't rise as you swing. Doing so will have the ball coming up elevated, thus giving your opponent an easy setup. You should keep your knees bent when you swing up until you hit the ball. Remember that rising is often an unconscious movement, so be sure to stay alert.

9. Don't face the front wall when you swing. Rather, you should stand parallel to the side wall when delivering forehand shots and at a 45-degree angle when delivering backhand shots.

10. Don't forget to hold your elbow at shoulder height.

11. Don't move your non-hitting arm in the opposite direction. Both arms should move in the same direction.

12. Don't pivot your feet at the same time. Remember to pivot your front foot to coil your hips and then pivot your back foot to uncoil your hips.

13. Don't raise your racquet or rush your swing at the last minute. Be sure to always be prepared for the swing.

14. Don't move too close to the ball, as this often results in a tendency to slice the ball. You should also avoid chopping down at the ball and strive to swing parallel to the floor at all times.

15. Don't hit the ball when it's too far back. You need to race back and strive to hit it when it draws even with your lead foot.

Most importantly, don't just read this list of racquetball "don'ts."

You need to put everything into practice and play the game the way you planned in the first place.

How to Find a Racquetball Coach

Sure, you can read a lot of materials about racquetball that can help you play a better game.

You could also watch as many training videos as you want in hopes of learning some useful techniques.

But, nothing beats finding a good racquetball coach who can teach you how to play batter and smarter.

Among other things, a good racquetball coach helps you learn the basics and essentials of the sport a lot more quickly than you would on your own.

A good coach also helps you avoid bad playing habits and provides you with much-needed motivation when you suffer from very slow progress.

Here are some useful tips on how you can find a good racquetball coach:

1. Ask your friends and other racquetball players if they know of a good racquetball coach. They, too, may be taking some lessons from a coach and could perhaps share a name or two with you.

2. Secure the names and contact information of your local professionals. If you don't find the necessary information online, try to search for a list of local racquetball courts or clubs and then contact them for information on your local pros.

3. Play in a few tournaments and then find out if any of the top players work as coaches on the side. It may not be a good idea to disturb them during a competition, but you could probably speak to them when they're in between matches. Even if they don't work as coaches, they may be able to refer you to a good local coach.

4. Attend racquetball clinics or camps. Not only will these intense sessions help you improve your game in a matter of a few days, but it could also successfully get you in touch with some of the best local coaches.

This is, in fact, a good way of meeting a number of coaches at once so you can choose which coach you can work with best. The other students may even be able to recommend a coach or two.

5. Take a lesson. As soon as you find some prospective coaches, it may be a good idea to start out by taking a single lesson with each of them. After each lesson, you should evaluate how well the coach handled the session, how enjoyable the session was for you, and how much you feel it can help you achieve your goals as regards improving your skills.

6. Once you've chosen a coach who seems best-suited to your style of play and who may be able to help you reach your goals, you need to start taking a series of lessons with that coach. Set a specific period of time within which you can assess how much the coach has actually helped in improving your game.

Remember that it can take some time for you to see significant improvements, so you'll have to be patient and objective when assessing whether the coach has indeed helped you or not.

It's equally important for you to follow your coach's instructions even between lessons so you can successfully strengthen the foundation you've built during the lessons.

If, after three months of working with a racquetball coach, you notice that you have gotten considerably better at the sport, then congratulations! You have found the right partner who can help bring your game to the next level.

How to Avoid Injuries

If you've played any type of sport before, then you understand that there are always risks for possible injuries.

Considering the speed of the games and the kinds of equipment used, it's easy to understand why racquetball can be one of the riskier sports out there.

The good news is that there are a number of effective ways to avoid all types of injuries that can possibly be incurred when playing racquetball.

Here are some useful tips on how you can avoid injury while engaged in the sport of racquetball:

1. Eye Protection

Almost all injuries incurred during a racquetball game have to do with getting hit by the ball in the eyes. The most common of these injuries are swollen eyes, lacerations, bleeding eyelids, abrasions, and bleeding in the eye sockets. This makes it all the more important for you to use the right protective eyewear so you can avoid these critical injuries.

Make sure you use goggles that are approved by the Canadian Standards Association and the American Standard of Testing and Materials.

2. Shoulder Protection

Shoulder injuries often result from using your shoulders in the wrong way during a game. The best way to avoid such injuries is to use the entire side of your body when you swing your racquet, rather than just your shoulders.

3. Elbow Protection

If you're familiar with the term "tennis elbow," then you need to realise that this injury happens to racquetball players as well. In order to avoid this injury, make sure you handle the racquet correctly and that you're using the right type of racquet with just the right mass. You may want to ask for the assistance of a racquetball coach towards this end.

4. Knee Protection

All that running and pivoting you do during a racquetball game can be tough on your knees.

This is why it's very important to engage in an appropriate stretching and conditioning program that can help strengthen your knees and keep you away from knee injuries.

And while you're at it, you may as well condition the rest of your body as well to make sure you're physically prepared to handle the challenges of the sport.

5. Feet Protection

Racquetball is one sport that keeps you on your feet. Your feet should therefore be strong enough for the demands of the game. Whenever you suffer from injuries such as ankle sprains, you can get sidelined for at least a week and even your personal activities may be disrupted.

If you play with the wrong footwear or with a new pair that hasn't been broken in yet, then you'll also be likely to suffer from calluses and blisters.

It's a good idea to break your new shoes in first before playing an entire round of racquetball in them. If you have old racquetball shoes, then you shouldn't throw them away before the new pair has been properly broken in.

The sport of racquetball is supposed to be fun. The good news is that you can let it stay that way by avoiding the most common injuries associated with the sport.

Pros and Cons of Joining a Racquetball Gym

One of the best things about racquetball is that it's easy enough to find a court, since there seems to be one in just about every park or high school gym.

The problem is that many of these courts are outdoor courts, which may not be ideal for when the weather isn't all that good.

If you want to have year-round access to an indoor gym so you can play anytime you want, then it may be a good idea to join a private gym.

Of course, you'll have to consider the pros and cons of doing so before you make a final decision.

Pros

1. **Convenience** – Paying for a full membership at a private gym gives you access not only to racquetball facilities, but also to a whole range of fitness facilities such as cardio machines and weights.

There are even gyms that have basketball courts, swimming pools, and saunas you can use as part of your membership. These facilities can help you get in better shape for racquetball.

2. **Facilities** – The quality of their courts is one of the best things about private gyms.

   They're generally clean and well-maintained, and they're usually located indoors, thus giving you a chance to play all year round.

   And because members are paying good money to use the courts, any damage to the playing surface is promptly fixed.

3. **Social Interaction** – A lot of private gyms have racquetball leagues and joining the league allows you to meet the other players and possibly establish new friendships. You could share insights and pointers with your fellow players to further enhance your game.

Cons

1. **Fees** – The price of gym membership is perhaps the most common complaint of individuals wanting to join a private gym. While the monthly dues at some establishments may be as little as $10, you'll likely be required to shell out a considerable amount to pay for initiation fees, which often run up to hundreds of dollars.

2. **Availability** – The availability of courts can be a bit tricky because some private gyms only have a limited number of racquetball courts.

   When you go to the gym during peak hours, you'll probably have to wait for other players to complete a match, even if you've scheduled an earlier playing time.

   To avoid such hassles, you may want to take note of the busiest times at the gym, which are usually the early morning, lunch time, and early evening. It's also a good idea to avoid going to the gym in the morning hours during weekends.

Before you join any private gym, of course, it would be wise to check out the public courts available in your area.

Who knows, there just might be one that can sufficiently provide everything you need in a racquetball court.

After checking out the public courts, if you still feel the need to join a private gym, then you need to make sure you join the right one that meets your specific preferences and needs. Don't be afraid to ask specific questions about a gym's facilities and what a membership includes so you can be sure your expectations are sufficiently met.

Printed in Great Britain
by Amazon.co.uk, Ltd.,
Marston Gate.